LEVEL 2

EASY PIANO SOLO

Easy Hymn Solos
10 Stylish Arrangements by Wendy Stevens

ISBN 978-1-4234-7793-8

HAL•LEONARD®
CORPORATION
7777 W. BLUEMOUND RD. P.O. BOX 13819 MILWAUKEE, WI 53213

In Australia Contact:
Hal Leonard Australia Pty. Ltd
4 Lentara Court
Cheltenham, Victoria, 3192 Australia
Email: ausadmin@halleonard.com.au

Visit Hal Leonard Online at
www.halleonard.com

AT THE CROSS

Words by ISAAC WATTS
and RALPH E. HUDSON
Music by RALPH E. HUDSON
Arranged by Wendy Stevens

Peacefully (♩ = 88)

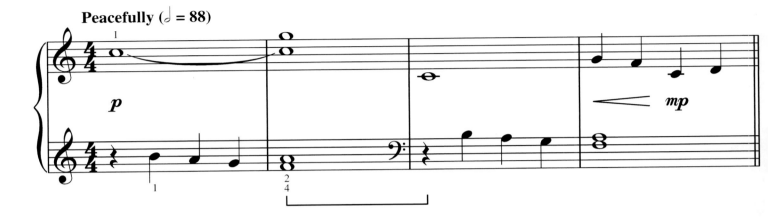

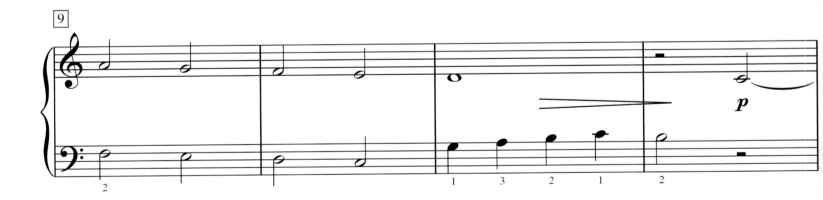

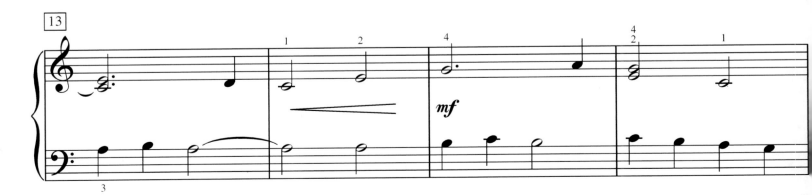

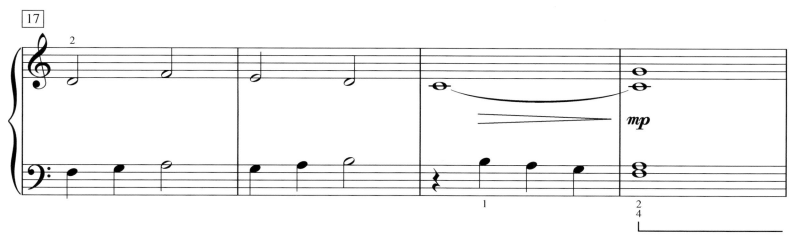

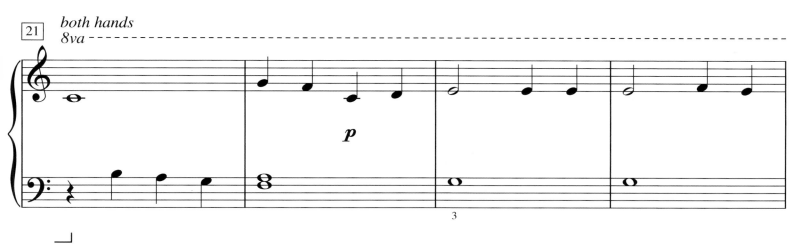

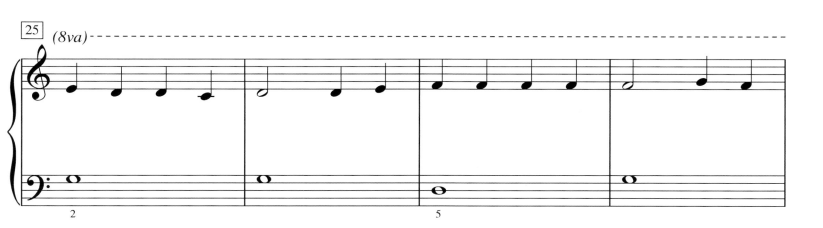

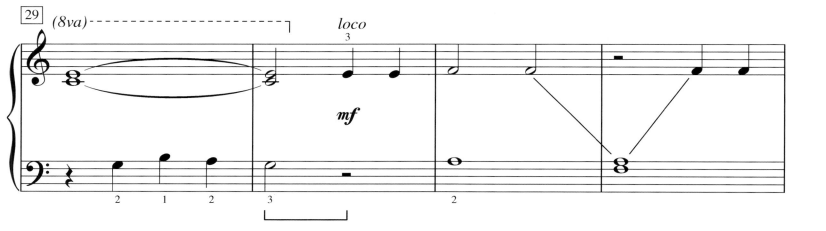

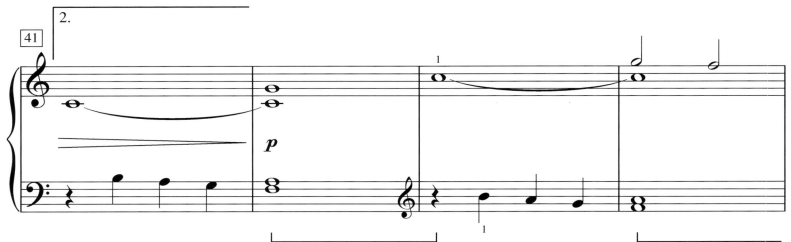

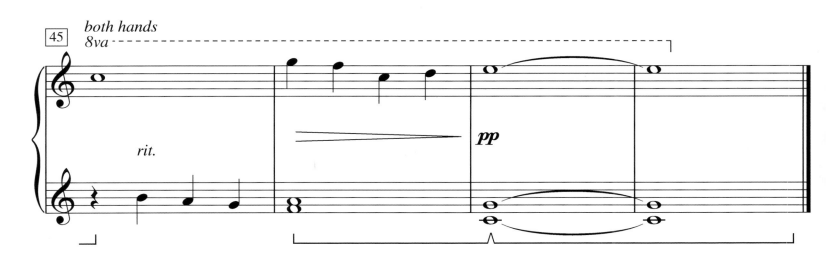

I'VE GOT PEACE LIKE A RIVER

Traditional
Arranged by Wendy Stevens

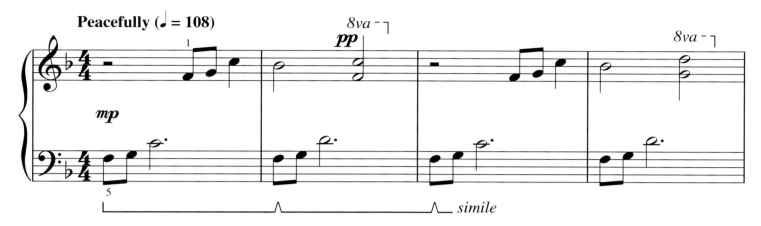

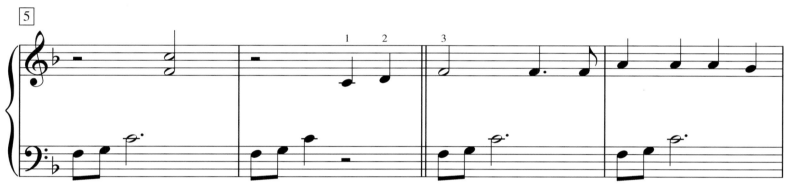

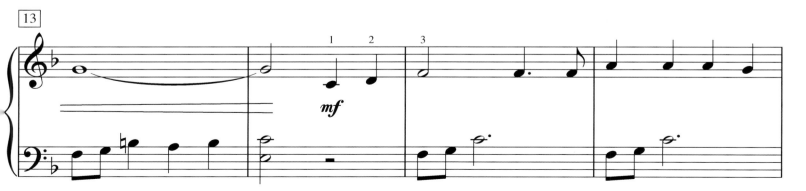

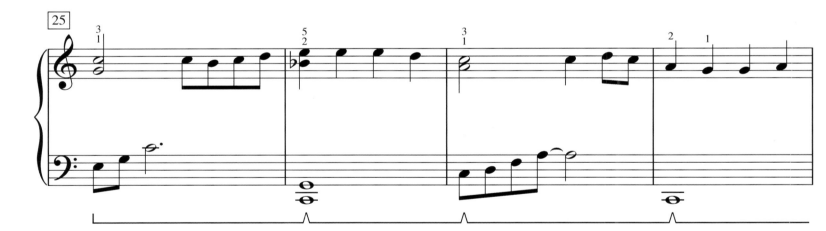

BE THOU MY VISION

Traditional Irish
Translated by MARY E. BYRNE
Arranged by Wendy Stevens

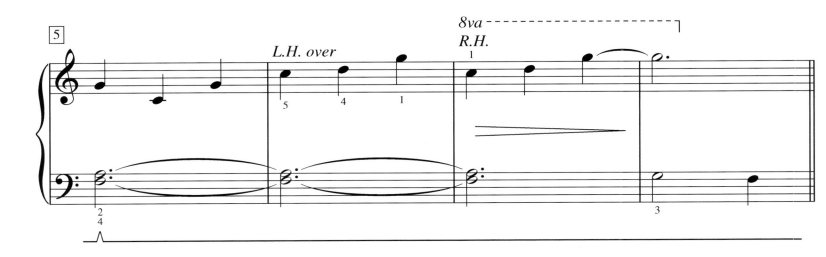

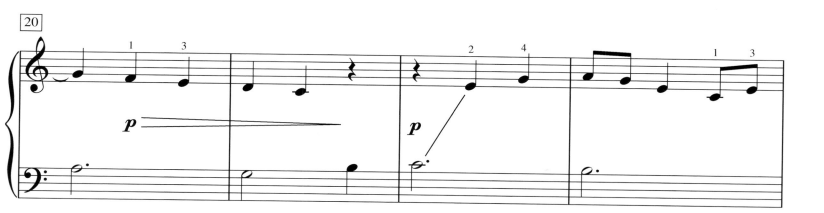

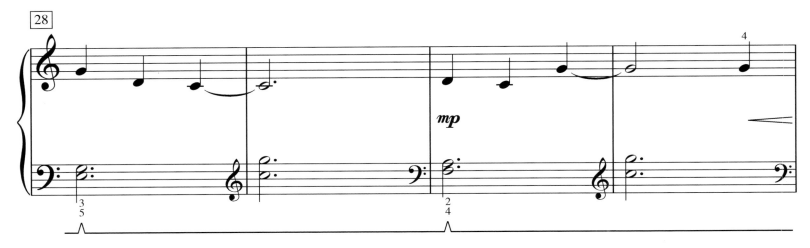

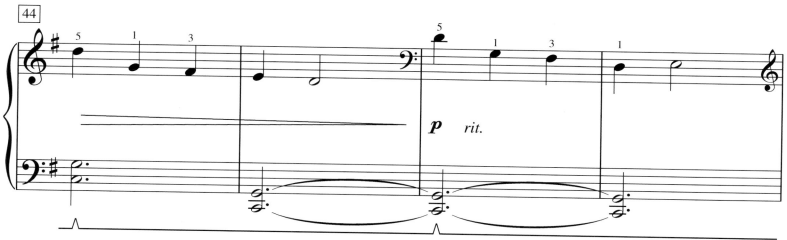

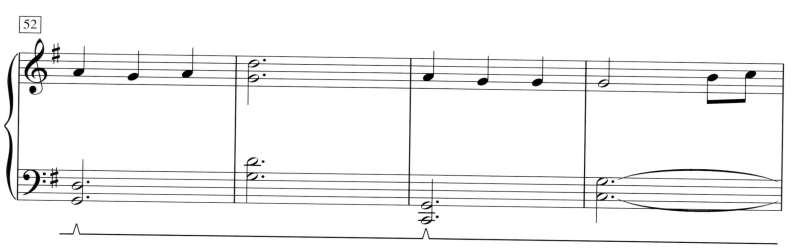

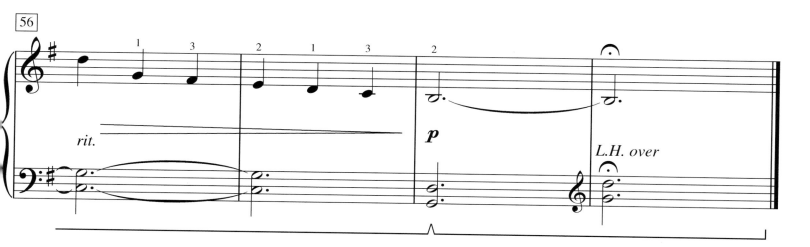

COME, THOU ALMIGHTY KING

Traditional
Music by FELICE DE GIARDINI
Arranged by Wendy Stevens

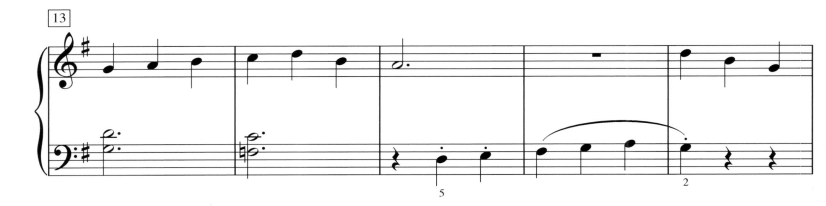

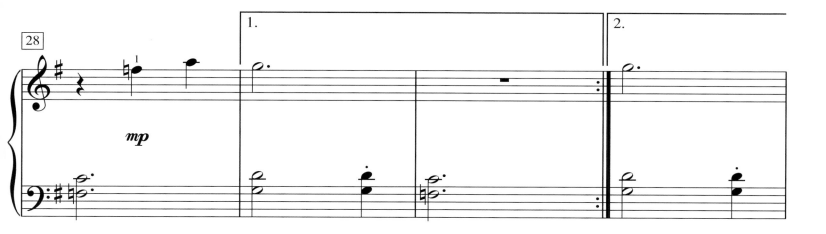

JESUS! WHAT A FRIEND FOR SINNERS

Words by J. WILBUR CHAPMAN
Music by ROWLAND H. PRICHARD
Arranged by Wendy Stevens

Joyfully (♩ = 144–160)

O FOR A THOUSAND TONGUES TO SING

Words by CHARLES WESLEY
Music by CARL G. GLÄSER
Arranged by Wendy Stevens

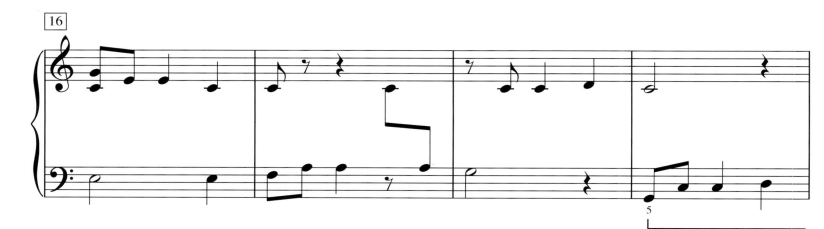

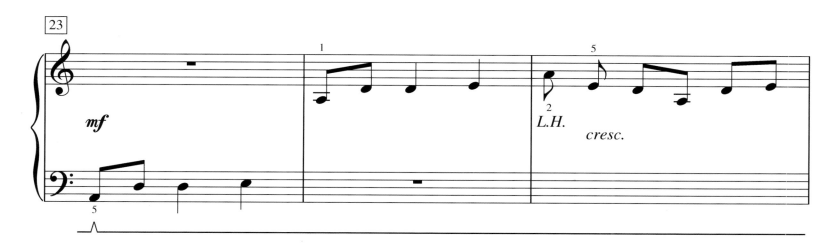

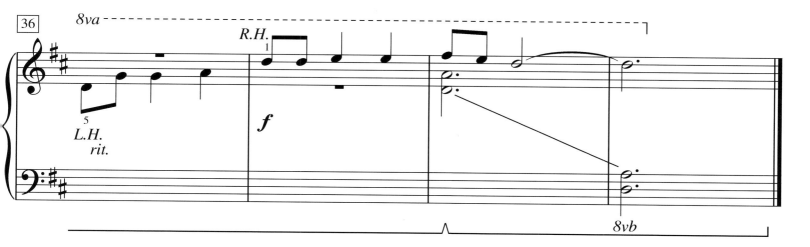

O WORSHIP THE KING

Words by ROBERT GRANT
Music attributed to JOHANN MICHAEL HAYDN
Arranged by Wendy Stevens

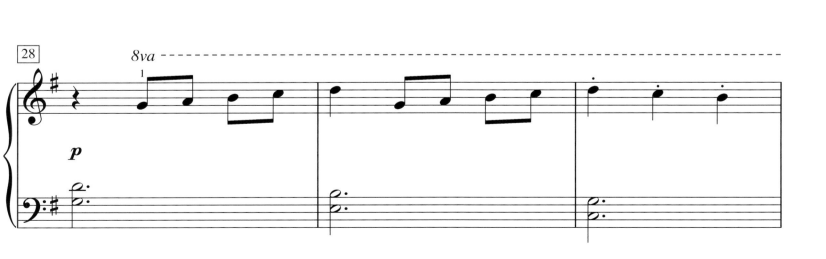

PRAISE HIM IN THE MORNING

Traditional
Arranged by Wendy Stevens

Spirited ($\bd$ = 92–100)

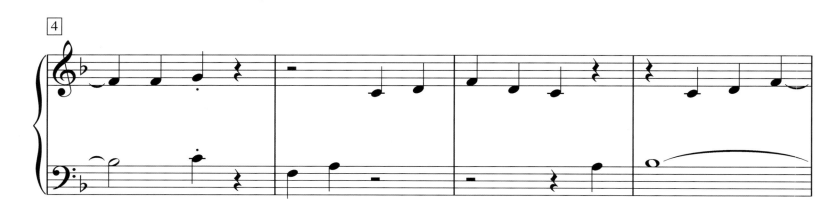

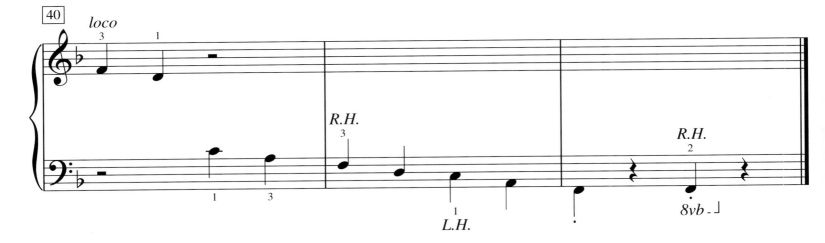

PRAISE TO THE LORD, THE ALMIGHTY

Words by JOACHIM NEANDER
Translated by CATHERINE WINKWORTH
Music from *Erneuerten Gesangbuch*
Arranged by Wendy Stevens

Boldly (♩ = 152–168)

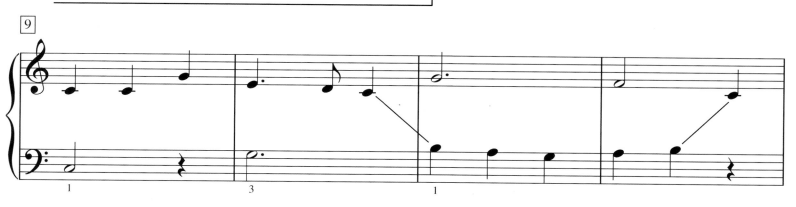

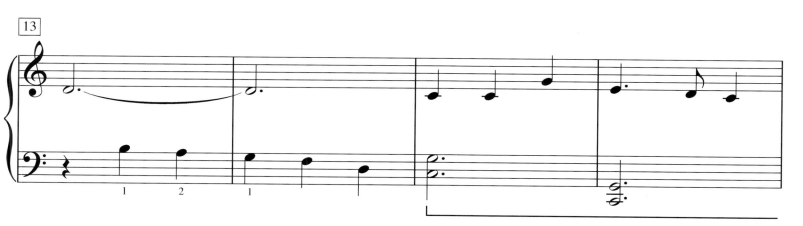

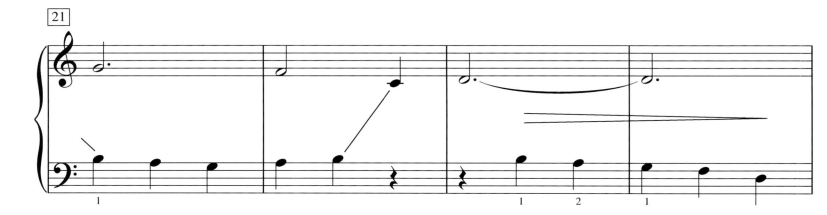

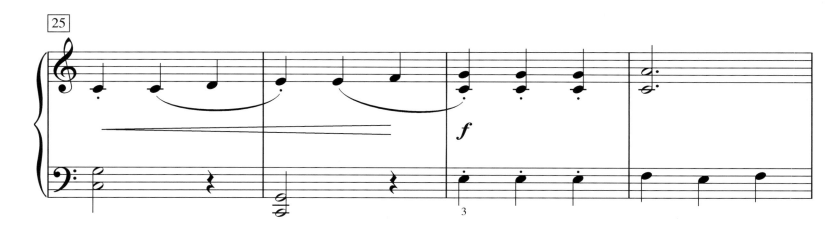

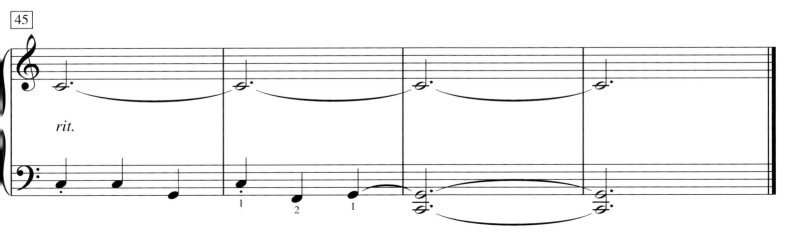

THIS IS MY FATHER'S WORLD

Words by MALTBIE D. BABCOCK
Music by FRANKLIN L. SHEPPARD
Arranged by Wendy Stevens

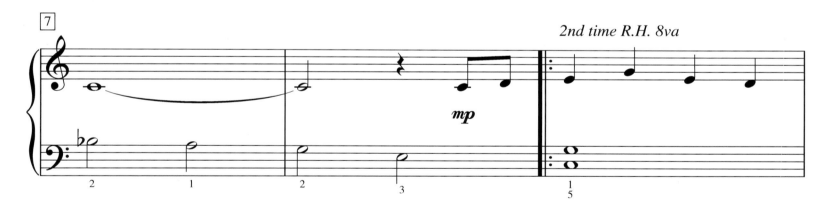

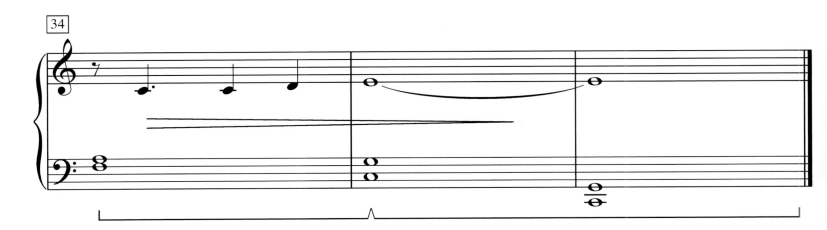